MATH SERIES

DIVISION

by S. Harold Collins

Book design by Kathy Kifer

Published by:
Garlic Press
605 Powers St.
Eugene, OR 97402

ISBN 0-931993-18-0
Order Number GP-018

www.garlicpress.com

To Parents and Teachers,

The Advanced Straight Forward Math Series has been designed for parents and teachers of children. This is the division book. It is a straightforward, sequenced presentation of advanced division skills. It assumes that basic facts have already been learned (if not, consult our first series: **The Straight Forward Math Series**).

These steps are suggested for mastery of advanced division skills:

- Give the **Basic Facts Review** (page 1) to assure competency in basic division facts. The test has 100 problems and is arranged to group facts (see Answers, page 29, for a display of facts).

  If knowledge of Basic Facts is not demonstrated, do not go on to the next level. Master Basic Facts first, they are crucial to division success in this advanced series.

- Give **Beginning Assessment Test** to determine where to start Practice Sheets. The Beginning Assessment Test (page 2) will tell which advanced division skills are sound and which need attention. Begin Practice Sheets where the Beginning Assessment Test shows that division errors start.

  Look at the Beginning Assessment Test. If you consult the Answers on page 29, you will see the problems are arranged in groupings. Each grouping is a skill. Each skill is sequential and requires mastery before a higher skill level can be started.

- Start **Practice Sheets** at the appropriate skill level as determined from the Beginning Assessment Test. Do not skip levels once begun; build to mastery of all skills.

  Practice Sheets are given for each skill level to provide ample practice.

  Set a standard to move from one division skill level to the next; either a percentage correct or a number correct.

- Give **Review Sheet(s)** appropriate to each section.

- Give **Section Diagnostic Test** as a final measure of a particular section. Section Diagnostic Tests are arranged to identify problems which may still exist with a particular skill (much like the Beginning Assessment Test).

  Set a standard to move from one section to the next. If that standard is not met, go back, focus on problem skills with Practice Sheets or similar materials.

- Give **Final Assessment Test** to measure all advanced division skills. Compare the change from the Beginning Assessment Test.

Contents

Basic Facts Review 1

Beginning Assessment Test 2

Section 1

Practice Sheets: Basic Facts, with remainders 3
Practice Sheets: 2 digits ÷ 1 digit, no remainders 5
Practice Sheets: 2 digits ÷ 1 digit, with remainders 7
Practice Sheets: 3 digits ÷ 1 digit, with & without remainders 9

Review Sheet 11

Section Diagnostic Test 12

Section 2

Practice Sheets: 2 digits ÷ 2 digits, with & without remainders 13
Practice Sheets: 3 digits ÷ 2 digits, with & without remainders 15
Practice Sheets: 4 digits ÷ 2 digits, with & without reaminders 17
Practice Sheets: 5 digits ÷ 2 digits, with & without remainders 19

Review Sheet 21

Section Diagnostic Test 22

Practice Sheets: 5 digits ÷ 3 digits, with & without remainders 23
Practice Sheets: 6 digits ÷ 3 digits, with & without remainders 25

Review Sheet 27

Final Assessment Test 28

Answers 29

$3\overline{)3}$ $2\overline{)4}$ $1\overline{)3}$ $4\overline{)8}$ $3\overline{)0}$ $2\overline{)8}$ $1\overline{)2}$ $8\overline{)16}$ $9\overline{)9}$ $10\overline{)10}$

$4\overline{)4}$ $3\overline{)6}$ $2\overline{)2}$ $1\overline{)2}$ $4\overline{)4}$ $3\overline{)3}$ $2\overline{)12}$ $1\overline{)10}$ $8\overline{)56}$ $9\overline{)27}$

$5\overline{)0}$ $4\overline{)12}$ $3\overline{)9}$ $2\overline{)0}$ $1\overline{)4}$ $4\overline{)12}$ $3\overline{)6}$ $2\overline{)2}$ $1\overline{)0}$ $8\overline{)64}$

$6\overline{)12}$ $5\overline{)5}$ $4\overline{)8}$ $3\overline{)12}$ $2\overline{)10}$ $1\overline{)5}$ $4\overline{)20}$ $3\overline{)9}$ $2\overline{)4}$ $1\overline{)3}$

$7\overline{)7}$ $6\overline{)6}$ $5\overline{)10}$ $4\overline{)0}$ $3\overline{)15}$ $2\overline{)14}$ $1\overline{)6}$ $4\overline{)40}$ $3\overline{)18}$ $2\overline{)6}$

$8\overline{)16}$ $7\overline{)14}$ $6\overline{)18}$ $5\overline{)15}$ $4\overline{)16}$ $3\overline{)3}$ $2\overline{)16}$ $1\overline{)7}$ $4\overline{)16}$ $3\overline{)30}$

$9\overline{)18}$ $8\overline{)8}$ $7\overline{)21}$ $6\overline{)48}$ $5\overline{)20}$ $4\overline{)20}$ $3\overline{)21}$ $2\overline{)18}$ $1\overline{)8}$ $4\overline{)24}$

$2\overline{)12}$ $9\overline{)36}$ $8\overline{)24}$ $7\overline{)28}$ $6\overline{)24}$ $5\overline{)25}$ $4\overline{)24}$ $3\overline{)24}$ $2\overline{)20}$ $1\overline{)9}$

$10\overline{)30}$ $2\overline{)8}$ $9\overline{)45}$ $8\overline{)32}$ $7\overline{)49}$ $6\overline{)36}$ $5\overline{)30}$ $4\overline{)28}$ $3\overline{)27}$ $2\overline{)12}$

$10\overline{)20}$ $10\overline{)40}$ $2\overline{)18}$ $9\overline{)54}$ $8\overline{)40}$ $7\overline{)42}$ $6\overline{)42}$ $5\overline{)35}$ $4\overline{)32}$ $3\overline{)18}$

Beginning Assessment Test

$2\overline{)15}$ $\qquad$ $4\overline{)21}$ $\qquad$ $3\overline{)60}$ $\qquad$ $4\overline{)72}$ $\qquad$ $7\overline{)98}$

$5\overline{)86}$ $\qquad$ $9\overline{)96}$ $\qquad$ $2\overline{)526}$ $\qquad$ $6\overline{)505}$ $\qquad$ $8\overline{)549}$

$10\overline{)90}$ $\qquad$ $17\overline{)88}$ $\qquad$ $52\overline{)786}$ $\qquad$ $26\overline{)956}$ $\qquad$ $37\overline{)925}$

$64\overline{)6,259}$ $\qquad$ $24\overline{)7,920}$ $\qquad$ $76\overline{)53,656}$ $\qquad$ $38\overline{)13,583}$ $\qquad$ $90\overline{)68,892}$

$714\overline{)44,982}$ $\qquad$ $233\overline{)94,973}$ $\qquad$ $446\overline{)88,560}$ $\qquad$ $540\overline{)756,000}$ $\qquad$ $251\overline{)176,955}$

Basic Facts

with remainder

$2\overline{)15}$ $3\overline{)8}$ $4\overline{)21}$ $5\overline{)18}$ $2\overline{)21}$ $3\overline{)14}$

$5\overline{)29}$ $2\overline{)11}$ $3\overline{)28}$ $4\overline{)35}$ $5\overline{)38}$ $6\overline{)15}$

$2\overline{)19}$ $3\overline{)20}$ $4\overline{)27}$ $5\overline{)29}$ $6\overline{)27}$ $3\overline{)1}$

$4\overline{)39}$ $5\overline{)32}$ $7\overline{)20}$ $3\overline{)25}$ $4\overline{)42}$ $5\overline{)47}$

$6\overline{)32}$ $7\overline{)5}$ $5\overline{)54}$ $6\overline{)27}$ $7\overline{)50}$ $4\overline{)27}$

$8\overline{)34}$ $7\overline{)64}$ $6\overline{)39}$ $9\overline{)30}$ $7\overline{)58}$ $8\overline{)66}$

$9\overline{)77}$ $6\overline{)58}$ $9\overline{)50}$ $8\overline{)83}$ $9\overline{)40}$ $8\overline{)70}$

3

Basic Facts

with remainder

$2\overline{)17}$ $\qquad$ $3\overline{)29}$ $\qquad$ $4\overline{)17}$ $\qquad$ $5\overline{)22}$ $\qquad$ $3\overline{)19}$ $\qquad$ $4\overline{)26}$

$5\overline{)29}$ $\qquad$ $6\overline{)32}$ $\qquad$ $7\overline{)26}$ $\qquad$ $4\overline{)37}$ $\qquad$ $5\overline{)49}$ $\qquad$ $6\overline{)29}$

$7\overline{)36}$ $\qquad$ $8\overline{)43}$ $\qquad$ $9\overline{)33}$ $\qquad$ $3\overline{)22}$ $\qquad$ $4\overline{)33}$ $\qquad$ $5\overline{)52}$

$6\overline{)37}$ $\qquad$ $7\overline{)41}$ $\qquad$ $8\overline{)50}$ $\qquad$ $9\overline{)39}$ $\qquad$ $6\overline{)45}$ $\qquad$ $3\overline{)25}$

$7\overline{)45}$ $\qquad$ $4\overline{)27}$ $\qquad$ $6\overline{)53}$ $\qquad$ $7\overline{)52}$ $\qquad$ $8\overline{)58}$ $\qquad$ $9\overline{)49}$

$5\overline{)54}$ $\qquad$ $9\overline{)61}$ $\qquad$ $8\overline{)60}$ $\qquad$ $4\overline{)39}$ $\qquad$ $6\overline{)59}$ $\qquad$ $7\overline{)66}$

$8\overline{)75}$ $\qquad$ $9\overline{)70}$ $\qquad$ $7\overline{)69}$ $\qquad$ $9\overline{)86}$ $\qquad$ $5\overline{)4}$ $\qquad$ $9\overline{)55}$

4

2 digits ÷ 1 digit

no remainder

2)22	3)39	4)48	2)36	3)45	4)56
2)28	4)60	3)51	3)60	2)52	4)72
2)62	3)63	4)68	5)60	2)74	3)72
5)75	3)69	4)76	5)70	6)66	3)81
5)85	6)72	4)92	5)95	6)84	7)77
6)90	7)91	8)88	4)88	5)80	6)78
8)96	9)99	4)96	5)65	6)96	7)84

2 digits ÷ 1 digit

no remainder

3)69	4)52	5)75	4)68	5)60	3)84
4)60	5)90	6)66	3)60	4)56	5)80
3)87	4)64	5)65	6)84	4)80	5)55
6)78	7)84	3)93	4)48	5)85	6)72
7)98	3)99	4)44	5)95	6)90	4)84
5)70	6)90	7)91	8)88	3)96	4)96
7)77	8)96	4)76	9)99	7)91	4)92

2 digits ÷ 1 digit

with remainder

$2\overline{)11}$ $3\overline{)17}$ $4\overline{)14}$ $5\overline{)32}$ $2\overline{)19}$ $3\overline{)23}$

$4\overline{)18}$ $5\overline{)47}$ $2\overline{)25}$ $3\overline{)28}$ $4\overline{)41}$ $5\overline{)62}$

$6\overline{)55}$ $2\overline{)47}$ $3\overline{)35}$ $4\overline{)54}$ $5\overline{)74}$ $6\overline{)69}$

$7\overline{)50}$ $3\overline{)44}$ $4\overline{)63}$ $6\overline{)76}$ $5\overline{)82}$ $2\overline{)53}$

$7\overline{)79}$ $4\overline{)77}$ $3\overline{)58}$ $5\overline{)94}$ $2\overline{)71}$ $6\overline{)82}$

$8\overline{)78}$ $7\overline{)97}$ $6\overline{)75}$ $5\overline{)86}$ $4\overline{)85}$ $8\overline{)90}$

$9\overline{)84}$ $8\overline{)99}$ $7\overline{)89}$ $6\overline{)94}$ $5\overline{)98}$ $9\overline{)96}$

2 digits ÷ 1 digit

with remainder

2)65	3)38	4)87	5)56	2)97	3)67
5)73	6)69	2)95	3)77	4)94	5)87
6)74	7)79	3)83	4)75	5)67	6)87
7)89	8)87	3)92	5)73	6)88	4)87
5)84	6)70	7)99	8)92	9)97	4)87
3)85	5)99	6)83	7)83	8)87	9)92
4)99	3)91	5)89	6)93	7)94	8)99

3 digits ÷ 1 digit

no remainder

$2\overline{)284}$ $3\overline{)639}$ $4\overline{)948}$ $5\overline{)480}$ $6\overline{)600}$

$7\overline{)336}$ $8\overline{)512}$ $9\overline{)972}$ $3\overline{)936}$ $4\overline{)228}$

$5\overline{)995}$ $6\overline{)210}$ $7\overline{)882}$ $8\overline{)872}$ $9\overline{)747}$

$6\overline{)804}$ $7\overline{)553}$ $5\overline{)285}$ $4\overline{)824}$ $3\overline{)984}$

$8\overline{)952}$ $9\overline{)990}$ $4\overline{)996}$ $5\overline{)905}$ $6\overline{)504}$

$7\overline{)966}$ $8\overline{)768}$ $9\overline{)891}$ $3\overline{)741}$ $2\overline{)526}$

9

3 digits ÷ 1 digit

with remainder

4)211	6)947	8)909	2)833	3)968
7)570	5)728	9)683	3)587	4)915
5)372	6)395	7)975	8)549	9)948
9)787	8)988	6)905	7)335	5)872
6)424	5)796	2)977	3)739	4)867
7)971	8)652	9)838	6)838	9)690

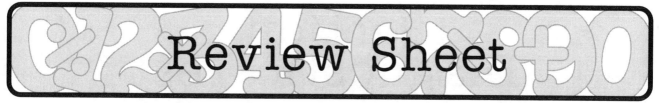

Review Sheet

Basic Facts, 2 digits ÷ 1 digit, 3 digits ÷ 1 digit

6)64   3)51   9)891   7)20   3)72

3)639   4)96   9)40   5)86   4)918

5)378   8)78   4)228   6)90   3)35

9)989   5)95   9)924   2)47   5)850

6)822   4)80   9)8   6)94   6)547

7)50   4)996   8)987   7)97   9)499

11

5)28   4)68   5)83   3)936   4)210

3)19   5)95   4)54   5)480   6)905

7)5   3)81   6)76   4)228   5)728

8)84   6)66   2)71   7)553   7)971

6)57   7)91   8)87   6)804   8)910

4)27   8)96   6)82   9)891   9)338

2 digits ÷ 2 digits

no remainder

12)60	15)90	20)80	13)91	11)77
23)92	16)96	10)80	22)88	25)75
17)68	21)63	30)90	28)56	12)96
15)75	40)80	19)76	14)84	18)54
23)92	17)85	29)87	10)90	16)80
19)95	27)81	24)96	26)78	13)65

2 digits ÷ 2 digits

with remainder

15)96 20)74 11)45 24)98 17)58

25)83 10)87 16)97 15)50 12)90

22)92 13)70 21)96 18)77 11)73

20)90 23)51 29)89 35)75 14)92

15)81 22)99 13)66 19)98 17)88

33)85 26)49 18)91 20)93 16)66

3 digits ÷ 2 digits

with and without remainder

$20\overline{)480}$ $25\overline{)351}$ $22\overline{)687}$ $35\overline{)354}$ $37\overline{)925}$

$40\overline{)880}$ $23\overline{)594}$ $33\overline{)957}$ $42\overline{)970}$ $31\overline{)427}$

$55\overline{)889}$ $24\overline{)989}$ $30\overline{)810}$ $28\overline{)825}$ $52\overline{)988}$

$47\overline{)947}$ $36\overline{)874}$ $21\overline{)966}$ $55\overline{)998}$ $48\overline{)730}$

$57\overline{)970}$ $44\overline{)880}$ $30\overline{)700}$ $23\overline{)828}$ $18\overline{)936}$

$10\overline{)872}$ $50\overline{)999}$ $43\overline{)820}$ $15\overline{)960}$ $34\overline{)920}$

3 digits ÷ 2 digits

with and without remainder

$60\overline{)720}$ $44\overline{)890}$ $62\overline{)832}$ $32\overline{)786}$ $58\overline{)936}$

$39\overline{)947}$ $50\overline{)950}$ $24\overline{)896}$ $72\overline{)936}$ $61\overline{)980}$

$25\overline{)741}$ $43\overline{)989}$ $82\overline{)937}$ $92\overline{)999}$ $19\overline{)893}$

$37\overline{)925}$ $28\overline{)928}$ $41\overline{)820}$ $52\overline{)786}$ $70\overline{)980}$

$15\overline{)874}$ $20\overline{)771}$ $34\overline{)816}$ $90\overline{)986}$ $61\overline{)976}$

$40\overline{)960}$ $18\overline{)674}$ $54\overline{)972}$ $75\overline{)975}$ $26\overline{)956}$

4 digits ÷ 2 digits

with and without remainder

50)2,250   41)1,450   29)2,436   78)6,890   31)2,356

46)4,527   23)4,830   40)3,900   81)3,807   16)4,827

52)1,700   90)6,480   58)5,850   24)7,920   62)2,984

37)8,658   29)9,240   35)7,000   23)9,862   80)8,782

75)8,427   49)9,008   19)9,158   56)8,252   64)6,259

4 digits ÷ 2 digits

with and without remainder

$60\overline{)9{,}420}$ $75\overline{)9{,}608}$ $14\overline{)5{,}572}$ $92\overline{)7{,}912}$ $37\overline{)9{,}999}$

$26\overline{)9{,}480}$ $43\overline{)9{,}331}$ $70\overline{)9{,}950}$ $38\overline{)8{,}474}$ $97\overline{)9{,}404}$

$62\overline{)4{,}900}$ $49\overline{)9{,}960}$ $17\overline{)8{,}900}$ $83\overline{)9{,}960}$ $35\overline{)9{,}645}$

$28\overline{)7{,}548}$ $73\overline{)5{,}402}$ $56\overline{)9{,}968}$ $34\overline{)7{,}301}$ $44\overline{)8{,}579}$

$20\overline{)8{,}740}$ $88\overline{)7{,}850}$ $67\overline{)8{,}752}$ $18\overline{)7{,}128}$ $39\overline{)6{,}000}$

5 digits ÷ 2 digits

$55\overline{)32,450}$ $30\overline{)15,900}$ $42\overline{)10,000}$ $23\overline{)13,892}$ $95\overline{)42,901}$

$67\overline{)22,378}$ $29\overline{)21,569}$ $70\overline{)58,089}$ $62\overline{)48,360}$ $38\overline{)13,583}$

$85\overline{)92,727}$ $44\overline{)24,791}$ $72\overline{)89,496}$ $26\overline{)85,000}$ $81\overline{)77,077}$

$52\overline{)31,200}$ $67\overline{)92,929}$ $48\overline{)56,261}$ $34\overline{)90,930}$ $76\overline{)53,653}$

$90\overline{)68,892}$ $19\overline{)46,854}$ $53\overline{)18,496}$ $88\overline{)60,900}$ $37\overline{)20,424}$

5 digits ÷ 2 digits

30)94,786   91)82,628   72)80,700   38)16,296   43)98,685

66)57,062   40)28,360   99)98,427   56)62,551   78)50,154

27)63,666   84)98,323   65)56,968   90)78,967   19)40,701

58)52,927   36)93,132   72)54,936   49)52,900   86)31,648

24)78,912   80)79,759   61)91,555   37)88,319   43)86,406

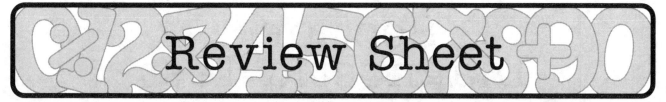

Review Sheet

2 digits ÷ 2 digits, 3 digits ÷ 2 digits, 4 digits ÷ 2 digits, 5 digits ÷ 2 digits

19)95   31)427   14)92   52)988

13)66   35)7,000   29)87   75)8,427

38)8,474   23)828   34)7,301   20)771

62)4,900   30)15,800   95)42,901   37)88,319

72)54,936   18)7,128   34)7,301   61)91,555

17)85   21)96   23)92   15)81

40)880   32)786   61)976   56)999

35)7,000   88)7,850   29)2,436   44)8,579

62)48,360   72)80,700   90)68,850   49)52,900

56)9,968   67)8,752   43)98,685   19)61,710

5 digits ÷ 3 digits

with and without remainder

308)46,278   478)85,900   233)94,831   521)86,708

139)67,276   691)60,549   275)81,400   380)97,307

882)56,448   547)70,000   117)68,094   666)98,689

452)93,564   773)60,356   422)79,643   362)92,672

906)65,293   284)96,400   714)44,982   589)86,583

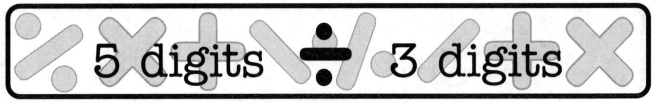

5 digits ÷ 3 digits

with and without remainder

341)87,000   250)95,500   701)64,549   417)98,927

737)43,746   524)87,508   233)94,973   837)79,439

362)91,000   674)58,792   902)66,008   434)99,386

268)94,977   574)38,500   309)88,374   680)40,187

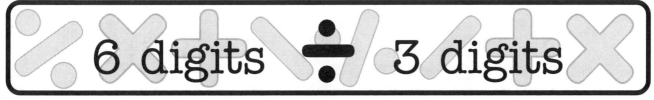
187)100,232   583)413,499   406)371,753   820)538,740

323)272,499   637)555,555   251)176,955   738)477,500

446)383,560   509)309,981   923)800,000   692)641,946

811)702,010   372)203,112   458)415,864   540)756,000

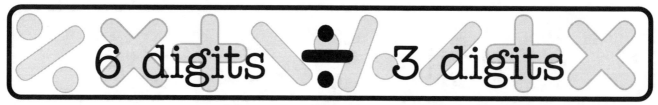
278)640,512   802)635,798   519)490,455   326)819,564

450)941,849   942)748,890   633)932,000   761)535,744

666)532,800   300)965,700   919)805,500   452)906,260

881)567,021   358)979,328   623)839,804   586)368,100

5 digits ÷ 3 digits, 6 digits ÷ 3 digits

400)57,800   730)925,200   482)46,754   248)93,000

633)931,776   546)25,983   342)712,044   349)97,022

460)978,800   890)155,750   575)44,883   257)98,170

619)905,600   434)99,386   512)99,386   192)863,210

5)38   6)27   3)81   4)84   5)90

6)76   5)94   9)891   7)882   4)915

29)87   16)93   30)810   42)970   92)999

37)8,658   83)9,960   39)6,000   48)46,261   72)89,496

250)95,500   701)64,549   342)712,044   692)641,950   547)896,721

ANSWERS

Basic Facts Review, page 1.

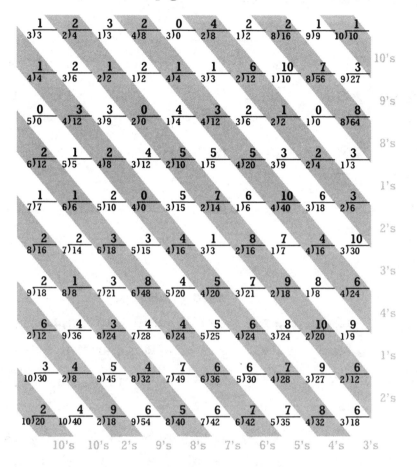

The **Basic Facts Review** has facts arranged diagonally. This diagonal arrangement quickly identifies facts which are firm and facts which need attention.

The **Beginning Assessment Test** is arranged horizontally by skills. This arrangement will identify skills which are firm and skills which need attention.

Beginning Assessment Test, page 2.

Basic Facts 2 digits ÷ 1 digit				
$2\overline{)15}$ = 7 R1	$4\overline{)21}$ = 5 R1	$3\overline{)60}$ = 20	$4\overline{)72}$ = 18	$7\overline{)98}$ = 14

2 digits ÷ 1 digit
3 digits ÷ 1 digit

$5\overline{)86}$ = 17 R1	$9\overline{)96}$ = 10 R6	$2\overline{)526}$ = 263	$6\overline{)505}$ = 84 R1	$8\overline{)549}$ = 68 R5

2 digits ÷ 2 digits
3 digits ÷ 2 digits

$10\overline{)90}$ = 9	$17\overline{)88}$ = 5 R3	$52\overline{)786}$ = 15 R6	$26\overline{)956}$ = 36 R20	$37\overline{)925}$ = 25

4 digits ÷ 2 digits
5 digits ÷ 2 digits

$64\overline{)6,259}$ = 97 R51	$24\overline{)7,920}$ = 330	$76\overline{)53,656}$ = 706	$38\overline{)13,583}$ = 357 R17	$90\overline{)68,892}$ = 765 R42

5 digits ÷ 3 digits
6 digits ÷ 3 digits

$741\overline{)44,982}$ = 63	$233\overline{)94,973}$ = 407 R142	$446\overline{)88,560}$ = 198 R252	$540\overline{)756,000}$ = 1,400	$251\overline{)176,955}$ = 705

29

ANSWERS

Begin **Practice Sheets** at the skill level where errors first occur.

Practice Sheet, page 3.

7 R1	2 R2	5 R1	3 R3	10 R1	4 R2
5 R4	5 R1	9 R1	8 R3	7 R3	2 R3
9 R1	6 R2	6 R3	5 R4	4 R3	0 R1
9 R3	6 R2	2 R6	8 R1	10 R2	9 R2
5 R2	0 R5	10 R4	4 R3	7 R1	6 R3
4 R2	9 R1	6 R3	3 R3	8 R2	8 R2
8 R5	9 R4	5 R5	10 R3	4 R4	8 R6

Practice Sheet, page 6

23	13	15	17	12	28
15	18	11	20	14	16
29	16	13	14	20	11
13	12	31	12	17	12
14	33	11	19	15	21
14	15	13	11	32	24
11	12	19	11	13	23

Practice Sheet, page 4.

8 R1	9 R2	4 R1	4 R2	6 R1	6 R2
5 R4	5 R2	3 R5	9 R1	9 R4	4 R5
5 R1	5 R3	3 R6	7 R1	8 R1	10 R2
6 R1	5 R6	6 R2	4 R3	7 R3	8 R1
6 R3	6 R3	8 R5	7 R3	7 R2	5 R4
10 R4	6 R7	7 R4	9 R3	9 R5	9 R3
9 R3	7 R7	9 R6	9 R5	0 R4	6 R1

Practice Sheet, page 7.

5 R1	5 R2	3 R2	6 R2	9 R1	7 R2
4 R2	9 R2	12 R1	9 R1	10 R1	12 R2
9 R1	23 R1	11 R2	13 R2	14 R4	11 R3
7 R1	14 R2	15 R3	12 R4	16 R2	26 R1
11 R2	19 R1	19 R1	18 R4	35 R1	13 R4
9 R6	13 R6	12 R3	17 R1	21 R1	11 R2
9 R3	12 R3	12 R5	15 R4	19 R3	10 R6

Practice Sheet, page 5.

11	13	12	18	15	14
14	15	17	20	26	18
31	21	17	12	37	24
15	23	19	14	11	27
17	12	23	19	14	11
15	13	11	22	16	13
12	11	24	13	16	12

Practice Sheet, page 8.

32 R1	12 R2	21 R3	11 R1	48 R1	22 R1
14 R3	11 R3	47 R1	25 R2	23 R2	17 R2
12 R2	11 R2	27 R2	18 R3	13 R2	14 R3
12 R5	10 R7	30 R2	14 R3	14 R4	21 R3
16 R4	11 R4	14 R1	11 R4	10 R7	21 R3
28 R1	19 R4	13 R5	11 R6	10 R7	10 R2
24 R3	30 R1	17 R4	15 R3	13 R3	12 R3

ANSWERS

Practice Sheet, page 9.

142	213	237	96	100
48	64	108	312	57
199	35	126	109	83
134	79	57	206	328
119	110	249	181	84
138	96	99	247	263

Practice Sheet, page 10.

52 ^{R3}	157 ^{R5}	113 ^{R5}	416 ^{R1}	322 ^{R2}
81 ^{R3}	145 ^{R3}	75 ^{R8}	195 ^{R2}	228 ^{R3}
74 ^{R2}	65 ^{R5}	139 ^{R2}	68 ^{R5}	105 ^{R3}
87 ^{R4}	123 ^{R4}	150 ^{R5}	47 ^{R6}	174 ^{R2}
70 ^{R4}	159 ^{R1}	488 ^{R1}	246 ^{R1}	216 ^{R3}
138 ^{R5}	81 ^{R4}	93 ^{R1}	139 ^{R4}	76 ^{R6}

Review Sheet, page 11.

10 ^{R4}	17	99	2 ^{R6}	24
213	24	4 ^{R4}	17 ^{R1}	229 ^{R2}
75 ^{R3}	9 ^{R6}	57	15	11 ^{R2}
109 ^{R8}	19	102 ^{R6}	23 ^{R1}	170
137	20	0 ^{R8}	15 ^{R4}	91 ^{R1}
7 ^{R1}	249	123 ^{R3}	13 ^{R6}	55 ^{R4}

The **Section Diagnostic Tests** are specially arranged too. The arrangement helps to identify if there are still problems and for which skills those problems occur.

Section Diagnostic Test, page 12

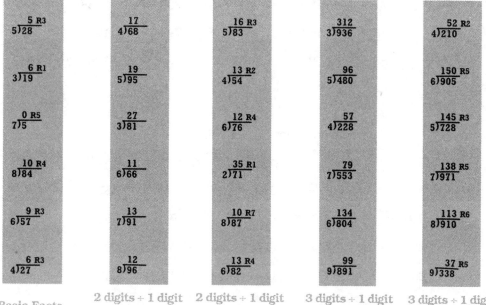

Basic Facts   2 digits ÷ 1 digit no remainders   2 digits ÷ 1 digit remainders   3 digits ÷ 1 digit no remainders   3 digits ÷ 1 digit remainders

31

ANSWERS

Practice Sheet, page 13.

5	6	4	7	7
4	6	8	4	3
4	3	3	2	8
5	2	4	6	3
4	5	3	9	5
5	3	4	3	5

Practice Sheet, page 16.

12	**20** R10	**13** R26	**24** R18	**16** R8
24 R11	**19**	**37** R8	**13**	**16** R4
29 R16	**23**	**11** R35	**10** R79	**47**
25	**33** R4	**20**	**15** R6	**14**
58 R4	**38** R11	**24**	**10** R86	**16**
24	**37** R8	**18**	**13**	**36** R20

Practice Sheet, page 14.

6 R6	**3** R14	**4** R1	**4** R2	**3** R7
3 R8	**8** R7	**6** R1	**3** R5	**7** R6
4 R4	**5** R5	**4** R12	**4** R5	**6** R7
4 R10	**2** R5	**3** R2	**2** R5	**6** R8
5 R6	**4** R11	**5** R1	**5** R3	**5** R3
2 R19	**1** R23	**5** R1	**4** R13	**4** R2

Practice Sheet, page 17.

45	35 R15	84	88 R26	76
98 R19	210	97 R20	47	301 R11
32 R36	72	100 R50	330	48 R8
234	318 R18	200	428 R18	109 R62
112 R27	183 R41	482	147 R20	97 R51

Practice Sheet, page 15.

24	14 R1	31 R5	10 R4	25
22	25 R19	29	23 R4	13 R24
16 R9	41 R5	27	29 R13	19
20 R7	24 R10	46	18 R8	15 R10
17 R1	20	23 R10	36	52
87 R2	19 R49	19 R3	64	27 R2

Practice Sheet, page 18.

157	**128** R8	**398**	**86**	**270** R9
364 R16	**217**	**142** R10	**223**	**96** R92
79 R2	**203** R13	**523** R9	**120**	**275** R20
269 R16	**74**	**178**	**214** R25	**194** R43
437	**89** R18	**130** R42	**396**	**153** R33

Practice Sheet, page 19.

590	530	238 R4	604	451 R56
334	743 R22	829 R59	780	357 R17
1090 R77	563 R19	1243	3269 R6	951 R46
600	1387	1172 R5	2674 R14	705 R73
765 R42	2466	348 R52	692 R4	552

ANSWERS

Practice Sheet, page 20.

3159 R16	908	1120 R60	428 R32	2295
864 R38	709	994 R21	1116 R55	643
2358	1170 R43	876 R28	877 R37	2142 R3
912 R31	2587	763	1079 R29	368
3288	996 R79	1500 R55	2387	2009 R19

Review Sheet, page 21.

5	13 R24	6 R8	19
5 R1	200	3	112 R27
223	36	214 R25	38 R11
79 R2	526 R20	451 R56	2387
763	396	214 R25	1500 R55

Practice Sheet, page 23.

150 R78	179 R338	407	166 R222
484	87 R432	296	256 R27
64	127 R531	582	148 R121
207	78 R62	188 R307	256
72 R61	339 R124	63	147

Practice Sheet, page 24.

255 R45	382	92 R57	237 R98
59 R263	167	407 R142	94 R761
251 R138	87 R154	73 R162	229
354 R105	67 R42	286	59 R67

Section Diagnostic Test, page 22.

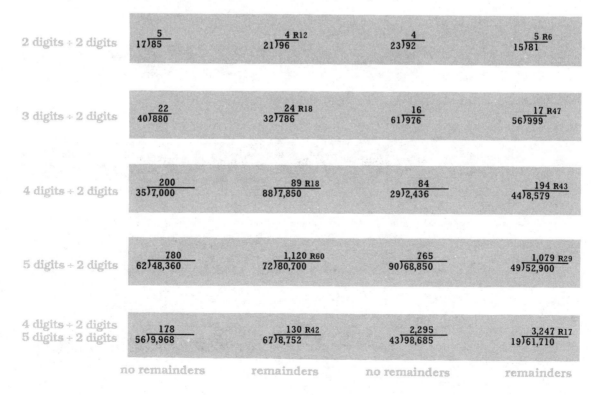

	no remainders	remainders	no remainders	remainders
2 digits ÷ 2 digits	5 / 17)85	4 R12 / 21)96	4 / 23)92	5 R6 / 15)81
3 digits ÷ 2 digits	22 / 40)880	24 R18 / 32)786	16 / 61)976	17 R47 / 56)999
4 digits ÷ 2 digits	200 / 35)7,000	89 R18 / 88)7,850	84 / 29)2,436	194 R43 / 44)8,579
5 digits ÷ 2 digits	780 / 62)48,360	1,120 R60 / 72)80,700	765 / 90)68,850	1,079 R29 / 49)52,900
4 digits ÷ 2 digits / 5 digits ÷ 2 digits	178 / 56)9,968	130 R42 / 67)8,752	2,295 / 43)98,685	3,247 R17 / 19)61,710

ANSWERS

Practice Sheet, page 25

536	**709** R152	**915** R263	**657**
843 R210	**872** R91	**705**	**647** R14
860	**609**	**866** R682	**927** R462
865 R495	**546**	**908**	**1400**

Practice Sheet, page 26.

2304	792 R614	945	2514
2092 R449	795	1472 R224	704
800	3219	876 R456	2005
643 R538	2735 R198	1348	628 R92

Review Sheet, page 27.

144 R200	1267 R290	97	375
1472	47 R321	2082	278
2127 R380	175	78 R33	381 R253
1463 R3	229	194 R58	4495 R170

The **Final Assessment Test** is arranged horizontally, by skills.

Final Assessment Test, page 28.

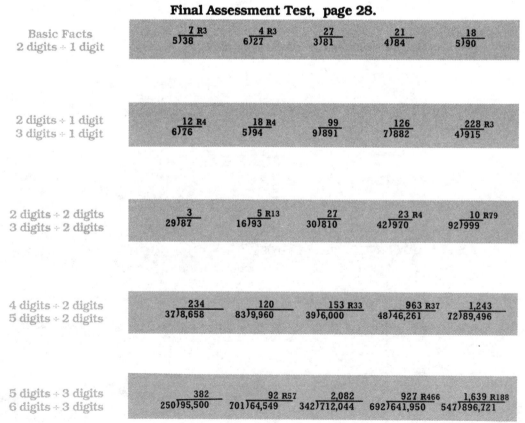

Basic Facts 2 digits ÷ 1 digit	$\frac{7\ R3}{5)38}$	$\frac{4\ R3}{6)27}$	$\frac{27}{3)81}$	$\frac{21}{4)84}$	$\frac{18}{5)90}$
2 digits ÷ 1 digit 3 digits ÷ 1 digit	$\frac{12\ R4}{6)76}$	$\frac{18\ R4}{5)94}$	$\frac{99}{9)891}$	$\frac{126}{7)882}$	$\frac{228\ R3}{4)915}$
2 digits ÷ 2 digits 3 digits ÷ 2 digits	$\frac{3}{29)87}$	$\frac{5\ R13}{16)93}$	$\frac{27}{30)810}$	$\frac{23\ R4}{42)970}$	$\frac{10\ R79}{92)999}$
4 digits ÷ 2 digits 5 digits ÷ 2 digits	$\frac{234}{37)8,658}$	$\frac{120}{83)9,960}$	$\frac{153\ R33}{39)6,000}$	$\frac{963\ R37}{48)46,261}$	$\frac{1,243}{72)89,496}$
5 digits ÷ 3 digits 6 digits ÷ 3 digits	$\frac{382}{250)95,500}$	$\frac{92\ R57}{701)64,549}$	$\frac{2,082}{342)712,044}$	$\frac{927\ R466}{692)641,950}$	$\frac{1,639\ R188}{547)896,721}$